# DK
## LIFE Stories

# MARIE CURIE

# DK
## LIFE Stories

# MARIE CURIE

by Nell walker

Illustrated by Charlotte Ager

**US Senior Editor** Shannon Beatty
**US Editor** Margaret Parrish
**Editor** Kathleen Teece
**Assistant Editor** Niharika Prabhakar
**Designer** Brandie Tully-Scott
**Project Art Editor** Kanika Kalra
**Assistant Art Editor** Simran Lakhiani
**Jacket Coordinator** Issy Walsh
**Jacket Designers** Brandie Tully-Scott,
Charlotte Milner, Dheeraj Arora
**Jacket Illustrator** Alessandra De Cristofaro
**DTP Designers** Dheeraj Singh, Vijay Kandwal
**Picture Researcher** Rituraj Singh
**Production Editor** Dragana Puvacic
**Production Controller** John Casey
**Managing Editors** Jonathan Melmoth, Monica Saigal
**Managing Art Editors** Diane Peyton Jones, Ivy Sengupta
**Delhi Creative Heads** Glenda Fernandes, Malavika Talukder
**Deputy Art Director** Mabel Chan
**Publishing Director** Sarah Larter

**Historical Consultant** Stephen Haddelsey
**Literacy Consultant** Stephanie Laird

First American Edition, 2022
Published in the United States by DK Publishing
1450 Broadway, Suite 801, New York, NY 10018

A catalog record for this book is available from the Library of Congress.
ISBN: 978-0-7440-2762-4 (Paperback)
ISBN: 978-0-7440-2763-1 (Hardcover)

DK books are available at special discounts when purchased in bulk
for sales promotions, premiums, fund-raising, or educational use.
For details, contact: DK Publishing Special Markets,
1450 Broadway, Suite 801, New York, NY 10018
SpecialSales@dk.com

Printed and bound in China

For the curious
www.dk.com

This book was made with Forest
Stewardship Council™ certified paper—
one small step in DK's commitment to
a sustainable future. For more information
go to www.dk.com/our-green-pledge

# Dear Reader,

It's not always easy to follow your dreams—and Marie Curie knew this better than anyone.

She grew up in Europe more than 150 years ago, at a time when it was almost impossible for a woman to pursue a career in science. However, in the face of many obstacles, she triumphed.

Marie is the first and only woman in history to win two Nobel Prizes for her discoveries in physics and chemistry. Her work helped lay the foundations for modern cancer treatment, which saves countless lives today.

Marie's story is one of determination and bravery. My hope is that whatever your ambitions, reading Marie's story will inspire you. If Marie were alive today, she would encourage you to feel excited about science and to make your own discoveries.

Happy reading!

Nell Walker

# The life of... Marie **Curie**

# A young scientist

**Hidden among the tall apartment buildings of 19th-century Warsaw, a little girl dreamed of changing the future laid out for her.**

The girl lived in a part of Poland that was under strict Russian rule, at a time when women and men were not treated the same. Women did not have access to the same jobs as men—and girls were certainly not supposed to daydream of becoming scientists.

For a woman, the world of science was almost untouchable—it belonged to men. But the little girl in Warsaw was determined to break into it and become a scientist. Her name was Maria Skłodowska—more famously known by the name she later took, *Marie Curie*.

This is Marie.

Zofia (far left) was nicknamed "Zosia"; Józef (second from right) "Józio"; Bronisława (far right) "Bronia"; and Helena (second from left) "Hela."

Maria had four siblings—Zofia, Józef, Bronisława, and Helena. The children of two teachers, they all went on to be scientists and educators—except for Zofia, who died when she was a child. Władysław Składowski, Maria's father, had encouraged his children's scientific curiosity from an early age, being a man of science himself. For many years he had taught mathematics and physics at a gymnasium.

**what is a gymnasium?** A European prepatory high school specializing in advanced education.

At the time of Maria's birth in 1867, Warsaw was in the part of Poland that was under the Russian Empire's control. For most of a century, Poland had not been an independent country—it was divided among Austria, Prussia, and Russia.

When Maria was a teenager, the Russian Czar Alexander II was killed by revolutionary students. Maria and her best friend, Kazia, were so happy to learn of his death that they celebrated by dancing on the tops of their classroom desks!

## RUSSIAN RULERS

A czar is another word for "emperor." Czar Alexander II was one of several emperors who ruled the Russian Empire in the 1800s. One of the Russian rules forced on the Polish people was the banning of the Polish language from schools, including in text books and in students' writing tasks.

During Marie's childhood, control of Poland was split among Russia, Prussia, and Austria.

Russian Poland

Baltic Sea

Prussian Poland

Warsaw

Austrian Poland

Maria and Kazia were happy because they felt that the Czar unfairly controlled their part of Poland. Life was not easy for most Polish people in Warsaw, and Maria's family—despite her parents' well-paid jobs—were no exception to this rule. Polish patriots, such as the Skłodowskis, were banned from openly expressing any pride in their own country. But despite this, Władysław Skłodwski still refused to follow the Russian rules, and he was fired from his teaching job.

what is a patriot?

A person who loves and supports their country.

Maria's father wanted his children to feel the same way he did about their home country, even though he knew it meant they could get into trouble. So, Maria followed in the footsteps of her parents—she became determined to show pride in her country, against Russian rules.

And this was not the only thing young Maria felt passionately about. Her childhood curiosity for her father's old lab equipment had planted the seeds of another certainty in her mind. Maria was going to become a scientist—no matter what.

"Life is not easy for any of us. We must have **perseverance** and above all **confidence** in ourselves..."

Marie Curie,
c.1893

15

# 2

# **Troubled** times

**As the Skłodowski family began to face serious hardship, Maria would find peace in her studies.**

After Władysław lost his job, the Skłodowskis began to worry about money. Once a well-to-do family, they realized they might not be able to afford the things they had previously enjoyed—such as good food, new clothes for the five children, and, of course, books.

The family of seven had little choice but to begin renting out the spare rooms of their house to boarders who Władysław tutored in exchange for money. But living in close quarters with strangers brought a new problem to the family. Illnesses became very difficult to avoid.

Caught from the bodily fluids of an infected person, such as cough droplets in the air, contagious diseases spread quickly in full houses. Unfortunately, in the 1800s medicine was not as advanced as it is today. Diseases that are now preventable, such as typhus and tuberculosis, were often deadly.

In just two years, Maria suffered the loss of her sister Zofia, who caught typhus from a boarder, and her mother, Bronisława, who died from tuberculosis.

## VACCINATIONS

During Marie's childhood, deadly contagious illnesses were widespread and caused millions of deaths globally. Today, doctors can stop people from getting many of these illnesses by injecting them with medicines called vaccines.

The deaths shook the foundations of the Skłodowski family life. Władysław was overcome with sadness, while his children wept in their bedrooms, mourning their mother and sister. Young Maria was devastated, but she was also a very resilient little girl. She put on a brave face—determined not to let heartbreak interfere with her studies.

Bronislawa
Skłodowska,
Maria's mother

Maria was only fifteen when she finished high school. She was such a bright student that she was awarded a special gold medal for her academic achievements. But her graduation was tarnished, because when the time came for her to accept her diploma on stage, she realized it would mean shaking the hand of the Russian grandmaster of education. Maria didn't think much of him!

DID YOU KNOW?

Today, most teenagers do not leave high school before the age of 18!

By 16 Maria had
finished school
and no longer
had her studies
to focus on.

However, despite her great achievement, the family tragedies and long, hard hours of endless studying finally began to affect Maria. After graduating, she became unhappy and withdrawn. At the time, doctors thought this might be due to "nervous exhaustion," but

## DEPRESSION

This is when someone feels hopeless to the point that they stop enjoying normal activities. Today, people can get help to feel better.

today we would probably recognize this as depression.

Władysław urged his daughter to take a year of rest and relaxation in the countryside. Maria took her father's advice. She spent many carefree months laughing, going to dances, and recuperating in the joyful company of her cousins, whom she loved very much.

As Maria's mood improved, she began to fall back in love with the idea of furthering her studies. It would not be long before she could return home, to her books and experiments.

# Studying **in secret**

**Back in Warsaw, Maria longed to attend university, like her older brother had done before her.**

At university, Maria could conduct her experiments correctly in a laboratory with all of the latest equipment. But there was one major obstacle standing in her path. Women were not allowed to study at the University of Warsaw. What would she do?

Like other girls at the time, Maria had no option but to attend night-school classes illegally at the secret "Floating University" of Warsaw. The university was so named because it needed to keep moving between the rooms of students and teachers around the city to remain undetected by the government.

A floating university was better than no university, but it wasn't enough. Not for a mind like Maria's. She needed the advanced teaching of Europe's world-renowned scientists at an official university. So, one day Maria and her sister Bronia made a pact. Maria would earn money to send to Bronia while Bronia studied at the Sorbonne University in Paris, France, which accepted girls. Once Bronia graduated, she would then do the same for Maria.

## THE FLOATING UNIVERSITY

In the 1880s, fed up with the lack of university education available to Polish women, teachers took matters into their own hands. Secret classes popped up in houses around Warsaw. These were organized into the "Floating University," largely thanks to the efforts of Jadwiga Szczawińska-Dawidowa (pictured).

The Żorawskis lived in this grand house.

Bronia left for France to study medicine at the Sorbonne. To help Bronia pay her tuition fees abroad, Maria took on several tutoring jobs—despite being just sixteen years old.

After several years of working as a tutor for various families, Maria realized she needed to save more money. She found a well-paid job as a governess for some rich relatives of her father, the Żorawskis, in the East-Central Polish village of Szczuki.

---

**What is a governess?**

A governess is a woman paid to teach and care for someone's children in their home.

There, she fell in love with Kazimierz, the Żorawskis' mathematician son. Kazimierz was an intelligent and handsome young man who shared many of the same interests as Maria. The two planned to get married—but the Żorawski family did not approve of their son marrying a poor relative such as Maria. They forbade it.

Kazimierz would go on to be a famous mathematician.

It was a great tragedy for the young lovers. Kazimierz never forgot Maria. Some say he remained in love with her for the rest of his life.

Maria (far left), Bronia (second from right), and Hela (far right) were close to their father (center).

Maria returned to Warsaw, where she filled the lonely hours educating herself through books and an advanced math course by mail. She was so good at so many different subjects that at first she was not sure whether to study literature, sociology, or science on top of the math course. In the end, she decided to study all three!

But she could still only conduct scientific experiments at home. Luckily, a cousin who worked in a lab helped her attend advanced chemistry lessons there in secret. Maria's access to the lab on weekends helped to grow her scientific knowledge. All the while, she never let go of her dream to attend the Sorbonne University, where she would receive the best training to be a scientist.

Then, there was a stroke of luck. Władysław Skłodowski was appointed as the director of a school, which meant that he could finally help to pay for his daughter's tuition. By the fall of 1891, after *years* of dreaming, 24-year-old Maria Skłodowska had enough money to go to Paris.

# 4

# **Paris**, at last!

**How long Maria had waited to come to this beautiful city—to join her sister Bronia and pursue her dream of becoming a scientist.**

Maria shielded her eyes from the sun as she stepped off the train, weary after her long journey from Poland. She could hardly believe she was here. Finally, there was hope. Finally, *eight whole years* since she had graduated school, she could dedicate herself to studying at a university.

Yet, as she wandered out of the station onto the bustling streets of grand Parisian buildings, Maria's excitement began to fade a little.

The crowd around her was chattering in the unfamiliar language of French. She realized she had a long way to go to fit into this new world.

Luckily, studying was what Maria did best. She would teach herself French, alongside the advanced science and math she would learn at the Sorbonne.

The Sorbonne is one of the oldest universities in the world—founded in 1253. It is located in the artistic Latin Quarter of Paris, where Marie lived as a student.

In 1891, Maria Skłodowska enrolled at the Sorbonne University. Fearing that no French-speaking teacher or student would be able to pronounce her name correctly, she quickly signed her name as "Marie" on the registration card. Just like that, she was "Maria" no longer.

At first, Marie lived with Bronia and her husband in a part of Paris called La Villette. Their home was nice enough, and the area pretty—but it was in an inconvenient location. It was a long trip to the Sorbonne each day, and the travel fare was expensive for a poor student like Marie. To make things harder, Bronia had a baby on the way.

Their apartment was already cramped, and Marie needed space to study without interruption. She preferred to work without the noise and distraction of others. She decided it was time to find her own place to live.

DID YOU KNOW?

The Sorbonne began accepting female students in the 1880s—just in time for Marie!

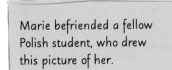

Marie befriended a fellow
Polish student, who drew
this picture of her.

Marie could only afford a small, dingy attic space on her small allowance, but it would have to do. The place she would now call home was at the top of a grueling set of stairs, winding its way up a tall, narrow house in Paris's Latin Quarter.

Her basic room had no hot water. It was furnished simply with an iron-framed bed and tiny wooden desk shoved together, and just a small window for light. The house's other occupants were mostly students, and they tended to keep to their little private rooms.

At university, Marie was behind her classmates because she had been out of school for so many years.

The fact that she was not a
native French speaker added
to Marie's insecurity that she
was not as good as her
peers—all of the lectures
were given in this unfamiliar
language! But she refused to allow
herself to remain behind.

DID YOU KNOW?

Marie would go on to
become the first woman in
Europe to gain a PhD—the
highest level of university
qualification.

Marie quickly learned to speak French. This
meant many lonely nights spent locked indoors,
glued to a desk piled high with French
dictionaries and science textbooks.

Marie would study and study, often into the early hours of the morning. When the oil lamp in her bedroom began to run low, plunging her desk space into gloom, Marie would gather books and hurry to the student library nearby. There, she would continue poring over mathematical equations, chemical formulas, and French vocabulary that eventually began to swim before her tired eyes. Sometimes, she would not even stop for sleep!

Constricted by how little money she had, Marie lived off tiny portions of radishes, buttered bread, and tea—not enough food for someone working so hard. Her once-rosy cheeks became ghostly pale, and her stomach often growled its complaint. Marie became prone to fainting from tiredness and hunger, but that didn't stop her. She was determined to excel in her studies.

"First principle: **never** to let one's self be beaten down by **persons** or by **events**."

Marie Curie,
*date unknown*

# 5

# A **scientific duo**

**Marie caught up with her peers, despite taking classes in a foreign language and surviving off only small amounts of food.**

All those hours spent studying alone in her attic paid off. By the summer of 1893, Marie had completed her master's degree in physics, and then a second master's degree in math. Marie was labeled an "outstanding student" of the Sorbonne and awarded a scholarship to continue studying.

**What is a master's degree?**

At university, people generally study for a bachelor's degree first, then a master's degree, and then a doctor of philosophy (PhD) degree.

The Society for the Encouragement of National Industry also asked Marie if she would be interested in conducting a specialized chemistry study, comparing the magnetic properties of different steels. She did not hesitate to say yes! However, she needed to find a laboratory space where she could conduct the work.

Józef Wierusz-Kowalski was Polish, like Marie.

Laboratories were rare and usually provided only to teachers. A former tutor of Marie's, the physicist Józef Wierusz-Kowalski, began to assist her in the search for a lab space. Józef said that he knew a talented and kind colleague named Pierre who might be able to help.

Pierre was respected by his fellow scientists.

Pierre was an experienced scientist, with many of the same research interests as Marie. He, too, was conducting in-depth experiments on magnetism. He worked as a professor at the Municipal School of Industrial Physics and Chemistry in Paris. Most importantly for Marie, Pierre had his own laboratory, thanks to his job at the school.

Word had traveled of Marie's outstanding talent in the field of physics. So, upon hearing from Józef that this talented young woman was in need of a space to work, Pierre did not hesitate before getting in touch. He said that he would be more than happy to share his workspace with Marie, and that he hoped they might conduct their experiments and discoveries together. So, in 1894, Marie began conducting her research in Pierre's lab. With the meeting of these two amazing minds, the world of science would never be the same again.

This photo of Marie was taken in 1892, two years before she met Pierre.

Marie quickly felt she could trust Pierre, and she respected his scientific ambitions. Like her, Pierre dreamed of making big discoveries. He was also a gentle and kind man, and he admired her exceptional abilities.

The two physicists began spending as much time as they could working alongside each other in the lab. As they conducted experiments together and discussed their findings, Marie and Pierre grew closer and closer. Pierre was glad to have a new companion, as he had been heartbroken for the past fifteen years over the death of his first love.

Pierre was older and a more experienced scientist. He was thirty-five, and she twenty-seven. But in Pierre, Marie had found an equal—someone who shared her goals, interests, and intellect. Despite getting along with one another, working in Pierre's laboratory was not easy for Marie. The lab did not have the advanced equipment that was needed for serious research and experiments— and there was not enough room.

Pierre's scientific curiosity was matched perfectly to Marie's, but he was also thoughtful—learning to speak Polish just for her.

But as Marie struggled to find free spots on the worktops for her equipment, she realized she didn't really mind. To be in this space with Pierre was a gift. They had begun to fall in love with one another.

Marie and Pierre became inseparable. As a pair, they were filled with excitement about the prospect of their future work together. What would they discover? What might they invent? The world of science was theirs to explore.

Pierre and Marie were a dream team, combining their knowledge to conduct experiments together.

Yet, there was a sadness in Marie that even Pierre couldn't help solve. She dreamed of home often. She missed her family in Warsaw terribly. And despite the happiness and excitement she had found, she wondered if she would ever feel at home in Paris.

Marie had strong opinions about the changes she wished to see in Warsaw. Back home, women were still not allowed to study science at university, and Polish language textbooks and classes remained banned in schools. Like her parents, Marie wanted, somehow, to make a difference. Marrying Pierre would mean settling down in France, away from Warsaw and like-minded people with whom she could fight for change.

Marie was not sure if she was ready to give up on a life in Poland for good. Feeling torn, she decided to take a vacation back to her home country, hoping this would give her the space and time to think. She wanted very much to be Pierre's companion for life, but it was a complicated decision. So, she and Pierre said a sad goodbye to one another, and she boarded a train bound for her home city of Warsaw.

While in Warsaw, Marie received a series of love letters from Pierre. They were short letters. After all, Pierre's skills lay in science, not in romantic poetry! Nevertheless, Marie could not help but be moved by his heartfelt words.

Pierre wrote of the passion he felt toward Marie. He told her that he missed her, that he believed in her ability, and that he looked forward to their life's work together. He promised he would wait patiently for her return to Paris, but that he would respect whatever decision she made.

With each letter, Marie's resolve strengthened. She realized that the love she shared with Pierre was something very special indeed. She returned to Paris, and the two were soon married—with Marie taking his last name, Curie.

Marie and Pierre had a small and modest ceremony, without frills or decorations, on July 26, 1895. Marie might not be able to change the situation in Poland, but with Pierre by her side, she could still achieve great things.

DID YOU KNOW?

Marie chose a dark blue dress for her wedding so she could use it as a lab dress after the big day!

# 6

# New **challenges**

**The summer they were wed, Marie and Pierre cycled through the French region of Ile-de-France—happy and in love.**

They would stop to look at the beautiful countryside and eat picnic lunches of bread, cheese, and cherries, then cycle on happily to stay the night at a nearby inn. Here, over bowls of steaming hot soup and glasses of wine, the two scientists would spend hours discussing physics and chemistry.

Pierre told Marie all about his latest work studying crystals, and she would tell him about her research on steel. Each would listen attentively to the other. Marie felt very content with the physicist.

Pierre was nearly a decade older than Marie, and so she looked up to him—she even called him "Boss" or "Chief" at times! But despite their age difference, Pierre considered Marie to be as intelligent and capable as he was. The newlyweds put their heads together to make exciting plans for the next year.

Marie and Pierre bought new bicycles for their honeymoon trip.

Marie was preparing for a fellowship competition at the School of Physics, which is where Pierre wanted to teach. The plan was to share a lab space, so that they could continue to work side-by-side.

They moved into an apartment on the Rue de la Glacière in Paris. It was very plain and had little furniture. There was a bed and a long, white desk for working. On the desk sat a humble vase of flowers, a petroleum lamp, and a pile of physics books. There were just two chairs, placed at either end of the desk: a seat for Marie and a seat for Pierre.

**What is a fellowship?**

A job as a "fellow" at a university, which comes with money for research.

Marie had always been a practical woman, but she wasn't used to running a home. Of course, she'd had little reason to, until now. But things were about to become more complicated. Marie gave birth to their first daughter, Irène, in 1897. Not fazed by the challenge of looking after a baby, Marie applied herself to motherhood with the same dedication she applied to her studies.

While Marie juggled her laboratory work with her tasks as a mother, a nanny would sometimes take care of little Irène. But Marie still found time to bathe her baby daughter.

### IRÈNE JOLIOT-CURIE

Irène Joliot-Curie would go on to follow in her parents' footsteps and become a scientist. She even won a prestigious Nobel Prize for her work in the field of chemistry. She was also one of the first three women to become a member of the French government and spoke about the importance of women's education.

Marie began working in a different kind of laboratory—the kitchen. She learned how to cook simple dishes, such as chicken and beef stew, to feed her family.

Marie loved Pierre and Irène very much, but the lab work remained incredibly important to her. So, day by day, she learned to balance her relationship with Pierre and the care of her young child with her career. Many husbands at the time expected their wives to remain at home, but Marie had the complete support of Pierre to continue her scientific work. He knew that his brilliant wife could do both.

"Giving up my **scientific work?** Such a **renunciation** would have been very **painful** to me."

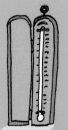

Marie Curie,
*date unknown*

It was an exciting time to be a physicist like Marie because of a number of new discoveries. In late 1895, a German physicist named Wilhelm Roentgen had discovered a fascinating type of "ray" that was invisible and could travel through books and papers— even through the human body, without being felt! These are now called radioactive rays.

Following Wilhelm's discovery, Henri Becquerel, a French physicist, noticed that uranium, a silvery-gray metal, also emitted rays. Henri wondered whether, in addition to uranium, there might be other materials that acted the same way. He got Marie wondering, too.

what is
a ray?

In science, a "ray" is a very narrow beam of energy, such as light

Wilhelm Roentgen noticed a material emitting (releasing) rays in his lab—which he called "X-rays." The rays could pass through material, such as skin, and he used them to photograph the bones in his wife's hand.

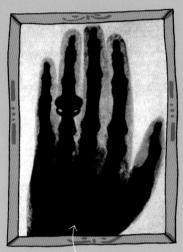

The first X-ray photograph

Henri Becquerel suggested that the newly discovered rays were released from substances without human interference, such as by heat being applied to the substances.

# **7**

# **Dangerous** work

**Marie could not stop thinking about Becquerel's discovery—the uranium rays. She decided to study them for herself.**

Marie needed somewhere to carry out her work. Luckily, her husband was able to help. He was still working as a professor of physics at the Paris Municipal School of Industrial Physics and Chemistry, and he once again invited Marie to share his lab. It was small and cramped, and she wasn't supposed to enter—but that hadn't stopped Marie before. She quietly and covertly set up the storeroom to use as her workspace. It was crowded with her equipment, and the darkness made it hard to see what she was doing. Mold collected in the corners of the ceiling.

Uranium

Still, Marie began her work with steely determination, eager to find out the secrets of uranium. To examine the element, Marie would use instruments such as an electrometer—which measures electrical currents emitted by objects.

Marie wondered whether uranium emitted rays by itself, or whether light, heat, or moisture might cause it to do so. She looked at whether the metal would release rays in the dark, and found that it did. So, light was not the cause of the rays! She pushed on with her next wave of tests.

In her tiny shoebox of a lab, Marie recorded the results from her experiments with great pride. Another metal, thorium, was thought to emit rays like uranium. Marie decided to experiment with this element, too.

Once Marie had exhausted her methods of testing the thorium and uranium, she was positive that she had discovered a new, special type of property, or behavior. She called this ray-emitting behavior "radioactivity." Might other metals be radioactive? Marie examined each in turn—but she could find no other ray-emitting substances.

## RADIOACTIVITY

Certain atoms (particles that make up matter) emit, or "radiate," energy. The energy produced is known as a "ray." Rays are high-energy waves that can damage the human body in large amounts. However, they are largely harmless in small doses, such as the amount used to take modern X-ray photographs.

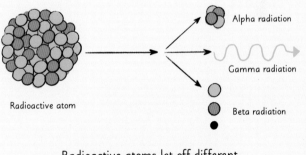

Radioactive atom

Alpha radiation

Gamma radiation

Beta radiation

Radioactive atoms let off different types of rays, or radiation.

In April 1898, Marie was able to publish her research on thorium's emission of "Becquerel rays." Marie had helped to establish an exciting new area of scientific research.

A number of other scientists began to assist Marie as she continued her quest to discover how radioactivity worked. Pierre, too, was fascinated by Marie's findings. The two joined forces to continue her work, a team once again.

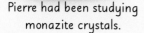

Pierre had been studying monazite crystals.

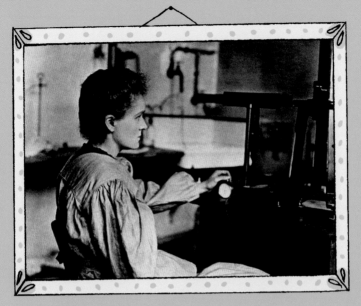

Marie spent many hours conducting lab work.

Marie knew the names of many chemicals and their uses.

# 8

# A **glowing discovery**

**Pierre had been studying crystals, but he put this work on hold to help Marie research the exciting new science of radioactivity.**

With the help of a few other scientists, the Curies began to hunt for other radioactive elements. Uranium is a derivative of the minerals pitchblende and chalcolite—and Marie had discovered that pitchblende gave off more powerful radioactive rays than pure uranium.

This captivated Marie. Could it be that there were other, unknown radioactive elements in the pitchblende giving off rays?

**What is a derivative?**

In chemistry, a derivative is a substance that is taken from something else through a chemical reaction.

The Curies needed to conduct further experiments, but the storeroom in which they worked was no longer big enough to perform the necessary

Pitchblende

tasks. It was agreed that Marie and Pierre would move their lab across the school courtyard and into an abandoned teaching laboratory. Marie thought it looked more like a shed! Still, she was excited to begin the next phase of their work.

Marie and Pierre needed to break down pitchblende into smaller parts, to discover any radioactive elements inside. They began by

dissolving pitchblende in a boiling-hot container of chemicals. Marie would then examine the sludge left at the base of the container to see which substances were there. The duo used an electrometer to see which of these substances behaved the most radioactively. The radioactive substances were then broken down further, and tested again for radioactivity.

DID YOU KNOW?

Marie named polonium after her beloved home country of Poland.

The results were astonishing and had the potential to catapult Marie's scientific career. She and her team had discovered two entirely unknown, radioactive elements.

The Curies published their results in 1898, announcing the existence of new "mystery elements." Marie decided to call the first element polonium. The second she called radium.

# THE PERIODIC TABLE

The periodic table is an arrangement of elements used by scientists. The elements are arranged in the order of their atomic number (how many atoms they have) or by their similar chemical properties. For example, certain gases are in one column, and certain metals are in another.

| H   |     |     |     |     |     |     |     |     |     |     |     |     |     |     |     |     | He  |
|-----|-----|-----|-----|-----|-----|-----|-----|-----|-----|-----|-----|-----|-----|-----|-----|-----|-----|
| Li  | Be  |     |     |     |     |     |     |     |     |     |     | B   | C   | N   | O   | F   | Ne  |
| Na  | Mg  |     |     |     |     |     |     |     |     |     |     | Al  | Si  | P   | S   | Cl  | Ar  |
| K   | Ca  | Sc  | Ti  | V   | Cr  | Mn  | Fe  | Co  | Ni  | Cu  | Zn  | Ga  | Ge  | As  | Se  | Br  | Kr  |
| Rb  | Sr  | Y   | Zr  | Nb  | Mo  | Tc  | Ru  | Rh  | Pd  | Ag  | Cd  | In  | Sn  | Sb  | Te  | I   | Xe  |
| Cs  | Ba  |     | Hf  | Ta  | W   | Re  | Os  | Ir  | Pt  | Au  | Hg  | Tl  | Pb  | Bi  | Po  | At  | Rn  |
| Fr  | Ra  |     | Rf  | Db  | Sg  | Bh  | Hs  | Mt  | Ds  | Rg  | Cn  | Nh  | Fl  | Mc  | Lv  | Ts  | Og  |

| La  | Ce  | Pr  | Nd  | Pm  | Sm  | Eu  | Gd  | Tb  | Dy  | Ho  | Er  | Tm  | Yb  | Lu  |
|-----|-----|-----|-----|-----|-----|-----|-----|-----|-----|-----|-----|-----|-----|-----|
| Ac  | Th  | Pa  | U   | Np  | Pu  | Am  | Cm  | Bk  | Cf  | Es  | Fm  | Md  | No  | Lr  |

Marie and Pierre hoped that other scientists would recognize their achievements by adding the two elements to the periodic table. However, this would not happen unless Marie found more proof of their existence.

She had yet to isolate radium and polonium—which means to find their purest possible forms. This would take many more hours of work, while fumes from the experiments burned her eyes. The fumes were so unpleasant that Marie began conducting her experiments in the courtyard outside their shedlike laboratory.

Marie and Pierre left behind notes and equations from their experiments.

The experiments were lengthy and demanding. Marie would find herself "broken with fatigue" when she got home in the evening. She would spend entire days stirring a boiling tank of chemicals with a heavy iron rod larger than herself.

Her health, along with Pierre's, was beginning to suffer from more than just the physical strain of their work. It was not known at the time, but the radioactive substances the Curies were constantly in contact with had the potential to be very damaging indeed. Neither Pierre nor

Marie noticed the link between their tiredness and the work they were undertaking. Nor did they make the link between the blackening of their fingertips and the radioactive substances they were handling without special protective gear. In fact, their hands would remain damaged for the rest of their lives.

They would not stop for anything. The duo was determined to reach their goal.

It took Marie and Pierre over three years to isolate just one-tenth of a gram of pure radium. Marie was ecstatic when she beheld her tiny miracle substance. The process was so hard that she would never manage to do the same for polonium.

Still, finally, after years of toil, they had succeeded in isolating a brand new element. And a surprise greeted Marie and Pierre upon entering their gloomy shed one night... the radium *glowed*.

Marie and Pierre couldn't wait to share their glowing discovery.

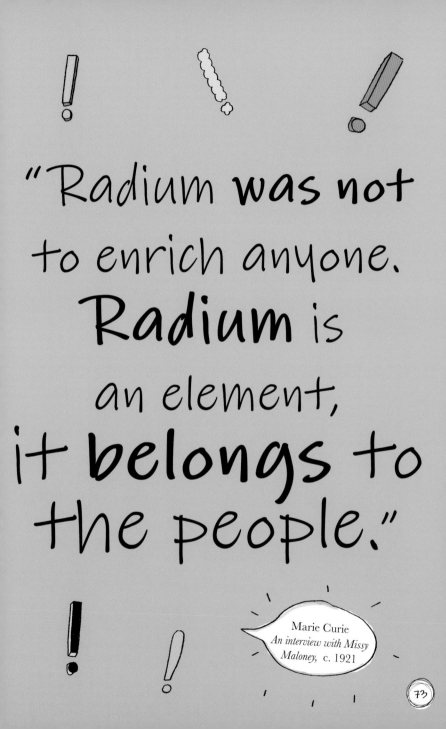

"Radium **was not** to enrich anyone. **Radium** is an element, it **belongs to** the people."

Marie Curie
*An interview with Missy Maloney,* c. 1921

73

Chapter **9**

# Triumph and tragedy

**The news about the Curies' discovery
of radium spread through the scientific
world and beyond, into the public eye.**

Soon, everyone had heard of Marie and Pierre
Curie. But, although universities in France accepted
female students, women scientists were still not
honored in the same way as men. Pierre was
nominated by French scientists for the Nobel Prize
in Physics along with Henri Becquerel, but this
would mean that Marie's crucial role in
the discovery of radium would not be
rewarded in an equally historic way.

**What is the
Nobel Prize?**

Founded in 1901, the Nobel Prize consists of
five prizes given to people who have achieved
remarkable things in their work, which help
humankind.

Soixième année. — N° 779.  Huit pages : CINQ centimes  Dimanche 10 Janvier 1904.

# Le Petit Parisien

## SUPPLÉMENT LITTÉRAIRE ILLUSTRÉ

TOUS LES JOURS
Le Petit Parisien
(DIX pages)
5 centimes
—
CHAQUE SEMAINE
LE SUPPLÉMENT LITTÉRAIRE
5 centimes

DIRECTION: 18, rue d'Enghien (10ᵉ). PARIS

ABONNEMENTS
—
PARIS ET DÉPARTEMENTS
12 mois, 5 fr. 50. 6 mois, 2 fr. 75
UNION POSTALE
12 mois, 5 fr. 50. 6 mois, 3 fr

UNE NOUVELLE DÉCOUVERTE. — LE RADIUM

**M. ET Mᵐᵉ CURIE DANS LEUR LABORATOIRE**

Marie and Pierre became so popular that they were featured on the cover of this widely read French newspaper.

Determined not to take credit for his wife's work, Pierre insisted that Marie be nominated, too. He wrote to the prize-givers, and in December 1903 the Curies were awarded a joint Nobel Prize for their research.

The couple traveled around Europe to give lectures and talks on their discoveries. However, they struggled to enjoy the trip.

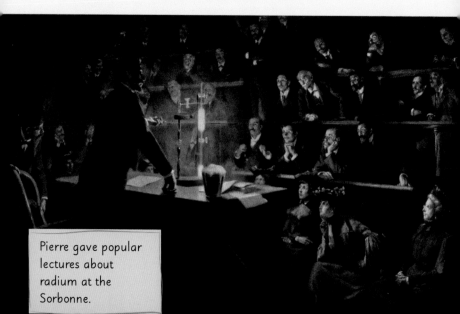

Pierre gave popular lectures about radium at the Sorbonne.

They had become worn down and unwell. The radioactive materials they were handling daily had affected their health, and Pierre was careful to note in one of his lectures that radium carried its dangers.

Back in Paris, Pierre took on a teaching job at the Sorbonne. By the time he began the work, he was so feeble he could hardly find the energy to teach. Still, despite their health problems, the Curies were delighted to welcome a second daughter, Ève, in 1904.

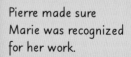

Pierre made sure
Marie was recognized
for her work.

Pierre's health continued to deteriorate over the next few years. He was often tired and distracted. One day in 1906, after a morning of work in the laboratory, Pierre walked across Paris in the rain to meet his publisher. When he arrived at the publisher's office, he found the doors locked and he turned back to cross the street. In his haste, he was hit by a horse-drawn wagon and was killed instantly.

Marie was devastated. No longer would she have her companion to work beside, to discuss ideas with, or to help raise their daughters. Only days before, the two had been excitedly discussing their lives together—the places they would travel to and their future discoveries.

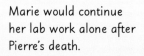

Marie would continue her lab work alone after Pierre's death.

Telegrams were sent to their friends and family, and Pierre's death was announced in the newspapers. Pierre would be missed by many.

The day after the funeral, Marie went back to work. Thinking of her husband, she knew Pierre would have wanted her to continue their research. Marie resolved to work through the pain of her loss, just as she had after the deaths of her sister and mother.

In the early summer of 1906, the Sorbonne made Marie an offer. They wanted her to take on Pierre's role as a professor. With sadness, but great determination, she said yes.

# 10

# A woman **undeterred**

**After accepting her husband's old teaching role at the University of Paris, Marie became the university's first-ever female professor.**

On November 6, 1906, in a lecture hall buzzing with excited students, Professor Marie Curie stood at the lectern where her husband had once taught. As she opened

her mouth to speak, no emotion could be read on the recently widowed scientist's face. Her voice was confident and clear— Marie was as focused as she had ever been. She delivered a matter-of-fact speech on the latest developments in physics to her rapt audience.

The constant doubt Marie faced as a woman scientist from fellow male professionals made her more resilient. Without her husband, she had to prove the importance of her research on her own. She would work twice as hard if that was what it took, putting aside her sadness at Pierre's death so that she could continue the work that had been so important to both of them.

But Marie had not forgotten her husband. She decided to create an institution, both in honor of Pierre and to provide a space where like-minded scientists might conduct their work in better laboratories. Marie pulled together the money she needed to build an institution from the ground up—in Paris, the city they had called their home. It would be named The Radium Institute.

In 1906, Marie also managed to find time to run what was known as a "cooperative school." This was a charitable school project that allowed

## THE RADIUM INSTITUTE

Founded in 1909, the Radium Institute was made up of researchers, physicists, a medical division, and, most importantly, a lab reserved exclusively for studying radioactivity.
It was later renamed
The Curie Institute,
and it now focuses
on cancer research.

The Curie
Institute

Marie with
Ève and
Irène in 1908

Marie's own children, Ève and Irène, to be
educated in a wide range of classes—including
math, science, history, and literature.

Childcare was challenging, with Marie being
so busy. Little Ève and Irène were often looked
after by Polish governesses while Marie worked.
They missed her deeply, but knew, even as little
girls, that their mother had an important job to do.

Marie showed a brave face to the world,
but she missed Pierre. The demands of her work as
a scientist and mother meant she had to keep her

pain inside, away from the prying eyes of the public and the curiosity of her young daughters. But when Marie found herself alone, as she often did at night once the children were put to bed and her books were closed, she would sit at her desk and find herself penning private letters to Pierre in her diary by candlelight. These letters helped Marie to feel connected to her husband and to summon the courage to keep going.

May 7, 1906

My Pierre, I think of you without end, my head is bursting with it and my reason is troubled. I do not understand that I am to live henceforth without seeing you, without smiling at the sweet companion of my life.

After years of fighting to have her work taken seriously, Marie achieved some remarkable goals during this time. Radium finally made it onto the Periodic Table. Her book, entitled *Treatise on Radioactivity*, was released in 1910. This textbook would eventually lead to Marie becoming the first person in history to be awarded a second Nobel Prize. Marie also defined a new kind of unit of measurement for radium emissions. This unit was named, appropriately, the "Curie."

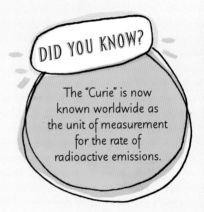

DID YOU KNOW?

The "Curie" is now known worldwide as the unit of measurement for the rate of radioactive emissions.

# 11

# War breaks out

**While Marie had been busy making discoveries and sharing them with the world, trouble had been brewing among the countries of Europe.**

In 1914, just when The Radium Institute was ready to start work, Germany declared war on France. By September 2, 1914, the first three bombs had fallen upon Paris. For now, the war was the most important thing on everybody's mind—the Institute's work would have to wait.

By this time, Irène was seventeen and Ève just ten. The Curie girls had been sent to Brittany—another part of France far from Paris—for the summer.

Left in the care of a governess and cook, they had been waiting patiently for their mother to join them.

Marie had planned to go to Brittany in August, but teaching and research meant she stayed longer in the city. Rarely in the habit of showing fear, Marie had comforted her daughters through letters when it began to seem certain that war would break out.

Dear Irène, dear Ève,

Things seem to be getting worse… I don't know if I shall be able to leave. Don't be afraid; be calm and courageous. If war does not break out, I shall come and join you…

If it does, I shall stay here and I shall send for you as soon as possible. You and I, Irène, shall try to make ourselves useful.

August 1, 1914

# WORLD WAR I

World War I lasted from 1914 to 1918 and involved many of the countries in Europe. In France, every man over the age of 21 was asked to join the French Army. The only men who didn't have to fight were those with certain medical conditions—such as Marie's mechanic, who suffered from heart trouble—or poor health, which would prevent them from being able to fight. Other exemptions included being a teacher or working as a priest for the Christian Church.

French soldiers fought in many battles, such as the Battle of Verdun, in 1916.

Marie promised her daughters that the war would end and that they would be safe. Meanwhile, she watched as one by one the men of the Radium Institute went off to war. By the fall of 1914, Marie and her mechanic were the only people who remained at the Institute.

Marie's most important job was to protect the single gram of radium kept for research in the French lab. It was precious because there was so little of it. The threat of destruction from bombs falling on the labs meant that Marie had to move the radium to a special vault in the French city of Bordeaux. So, she carefully placed the radium in a locked lead box used for transporting valuable elements and boarded a train to leave Paris.

Once the radium was
safely in Bordeaux,
Marie spent the
journey back home
wondering how
she might help with
the war effort.

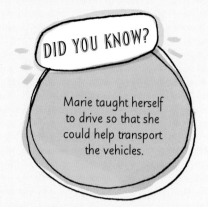

DID YOU KNOW?

Marie taught herself
to drive so that she
could help transport
the vehicles.

Many women contributed by becoming nurses
and caring for injured soldiers. But, in true Marie
style, she wanted to do more. Instead of donning
white medical robes, she turned to her expert
knowledge of radioactivity, and the recent
invention of X-ray machines. Known then as
"Roentgen machines," after Wilhelm Roentgen's
discovery, there were only a
small number in use.
Marie recognized how
important the X-ray
technology would
be for treating
injured soldiers.
X-rays would
allow doctors to

view inside injured soldiers' bodies to see shrapnel and bullets that needed to be removed or fractured bones that needed setting. Marie realized that portable X-ray machines could be taken to soldiers fresh off the battlefield. She set about gathering the apparatus to create as many as possible, and hundreds of radiology machines were built. These mobile machines, named *petites Curies* ("little Curies"), would be put to great use.

**What is shrapnel?**

Shrapnel is any fragment thrown out by an exploded bomb that could end up embedded in a soldier's body and need to be removed.

Because Irène was now 17 years of age, she was old enough to help her mother with the transportation of these vehicles. Despite having little experience working with X-rays directly, the Curie women set up more than 200 radiological units during the first two years of the war, between 1914 and 1916. They also invented a special training program to teach other women how to operate their machines.

The war ended on November 11, 1918. Marie continued to train American soldiers in operating the radiology machines. These young men were glad for the distraction, as they waited to return home to their country and loved ones.

Irène Curie was awarded a military medal in recognition of her important hospital work during the war. Together, mother and daughter helped to build and transport vehicles that would be used to treat around one million soldiers.

It had been an act of great bravery from the two Curie women. They would remember these difficult times for many years to come.

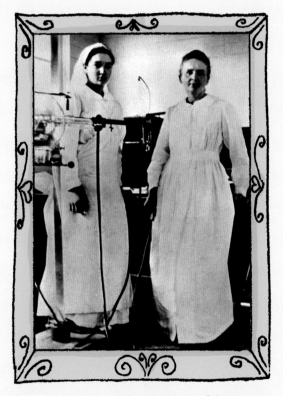

Shown here during the early years of the war, Irène (left) became her mother's (right) assistant during World War I.

# Chapter 12

# The girl with radium eyes

**The Radium Institute had patiently awaited Marie's return, and when the war ended in 1918, they welcomed her home.**

As ever, the Institute needed more money to carry out the work they had planned. Luckily, Marie Curie's work and war efforts had garnered the attention of several philanthropists and journalists who had the power to help.

Marie returned to teaching at the Sorbonne, alongside her work at the Institute.

## WHAT IS A PHILANTHROPIST?

A philanthropist is a person who seeks to support an important cause, usually by making large donations of money. One of the philanthropists who donated generously to The Radium Institute was Henri de Rothschild, a wealthy Frenchman who funded many scientific efforts and research projects. Henri would eventually become Irène Curie's collaborator and husband.

Henri de Rothschild

In May 1920, Marie decided to give an interview to a journalist in the US, Marie Mattingly Meloney. Marie Curie rarely spoke to newspapers and preferred to keep her life out of the public eye, but she realized that she could use the interview to raise money. The more people who heard about what she was doing, the more money might be donated to help run the Institute.

During the interview, Marie made it clear that while the Institute only possessed a single gram of radium, the research centers in the United States had 50 times this amount. Marie Mattingly Meloney was inspired and went away with an idea. She would organize a funding campaign to raise money for the Parisian research labs.

Throughout the 1920s, Marie Curie continued her own campaigning, raising awareness about the need for funding and laboratories. Tirelessly, she did this alongside her teaching work.

In 1921, Marie set out on a great tour of the United States, accompanied by her daughters. The Americans dubbed this aging woman, dressed plainly in black and moving slowly from exhaustion and age, "the girl with the radium eyes."

This is Marie.

The Curies and Marie Mattingly Meloney (far left).

Marie's presence in the US caught the attention of some very important people. On May 20, 1921, Marie visited the White House to receive a very special gift from President Warren G. Harding. He presented her with a gram of radium, divided up into 10 small test-tubes, which were sealed tightly shut. Marie would use this extra radium to continue her research back in France.

Marie with US President Warren Harding at The White House.

But by the time Marie returned home to France in the mid-1920s, she was physically and mentally exhausted. Only in her fifties, Marie appeared to be a much older woman. Her body was showing the signs of damage following long-term exposure to radium.

## A HARMFUL SUBSTANCE

In 1901, Henri Becquerel found that some radium had burned through his pocket and burned his skin. However, he did not guess just how damaging the substance could be. Exposure to radium over long periods of time can be very harmful. If it gets inside the body, it stays present in the bloodstream and bones. It increases a person's risk of developing cancer and can cause problems with their blood and teeth. It wasn't until the late 1920s that scientists linked radium with cancer.

Skin powder containing radium was sold before people knew its effects.

When it was first discovered, radium was thought to be a great treatment for cancer, as it could destroy the cancer cells.

Posters were made to advertise the use of radium in cancer treatment.

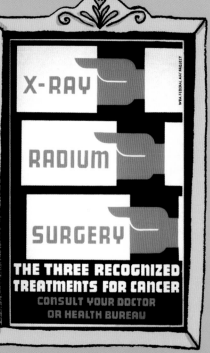

Among other ailments, Marie had developed cataracts. This eye condition causes cloudy vision and can lead to total blindness. Marie's misty vision meant that she had to write her scientific notes in very large letters. She also needed to be guided around by her daughters.

In the 1930s, now approaching her sixtieth year, Marie adopted a new, strict diet of fresh vegetables. She pushed herself to go on regular walks. She knew that something was wrong with her body and thought that this might help her get better. But it was too late—the damage had been done.

On some days, Marie found herself totally unable to go into her laboratory to work. She was becoming more and more frail as time went on.

Doctors tried to diagnose her illness, but they failed to identify it correctly. Instead, she was misdiagnosed with tuberculosis and sent to be treated at an infirmary in Switzerland. There, a medical expert suggested she might be suffering from a mysterious and incurable blood disorder— although he could not say what, exactly.

Marie continued to suffer with her health as the months went on, but nevertheless she returned to her work at the Institute in Paris. One sunny, midsummer day in 1934, Marie made her daily journey to the lab—not knowing

what is a diagnosis?

A diagnosis is the identification of a patient's condition or illness by looking at their symptoms.

it would be the last trip of its kind. She would not be able to muster the strength to return again.

Marie died on July 4, 1934, from a condition we now recognize as aplastic pernicious anemia, a disease of the blood similar to cancer. The aplastic anemia was caused by her exposure to very large amounts of radium over a long period of time.

Marie in 1930

The woman who won two Nobel Prizes was buried not once, but twice. First, Marie was laid to rest in Sceaux, France, beside her husband, Pierre Curie, and his relatives. But half a century later, Marie and Pierre were reburied in the Panthéon in Paris—France's national mausoleum. Marie was the first woman

Marie's final burial place was the Panthéon in Paris.

to be buried there, beside France's most accomplished and renowned men.

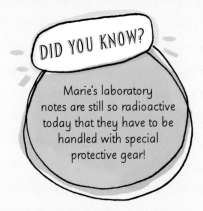

The young Maria made it her mission to step into the great unknown of scientific discovery. Marie's groundbreaking research in radioactivity has had far-reaching benefits on the work scientists and doctors are able to do today—when radioactive rays are used carefully in chemotherapy to kill cancer cells inside people suffering from the disease.

## MARIE CURIE CHARITY

The UK's Marie Curie Charity, recognized by its symbol of the yellow daffodil, was established in 1948 by a hospital that specialized in treating women with cancer. Today, the charity provides care and offers a better quality of life for dying patients. Donations help to support their nine working hospices.

Marie's life's work, carried out over a century ago, continues to serve as an inspiring lesson in the 21st century. Marie famously said: "One never notices what has been done; one can only see what remains to be done." She was referring to the progress of scientific discovery—but her words could also be about the progress of women in science. After all, if Marie had done what was expected of her as a girl in the 19th century, none of this would have happened.

# Marie's
# **family tree**

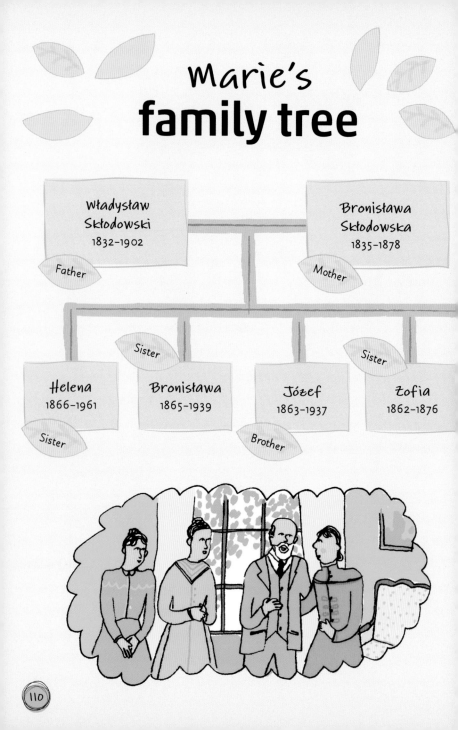

Władysław
Skłodowski
1832–1902

*Father*

Bronisława
Skłodowska
1835–1878

*Mother*

*Sister*

*Sister*

Helena
1866–1961

Bronisława
1865–1939

Józef
1863–1937

Zofia
1862–1876

*Sister*

*Brother*

Marie Curie
1867–1934

Pierre Curie
1859–1906

Husband

Marie loved her little family greatly.

Irène Joliot-Curie
1897–1956

Daughter

Ève Curie
1904–2007

Daughter

# Timeline

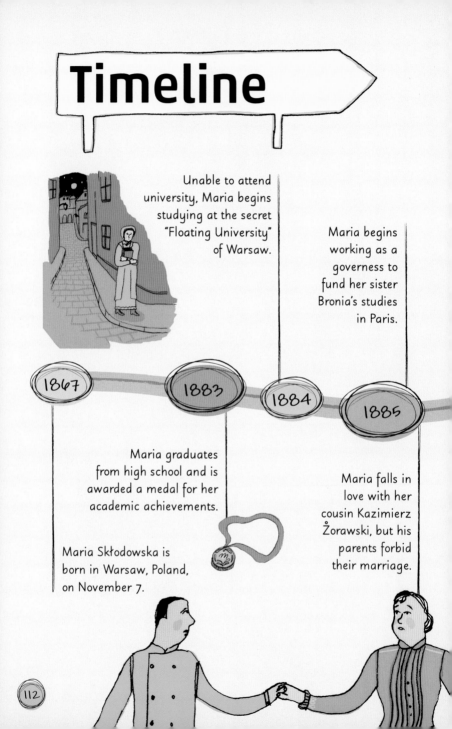

Unable to attend university, Maria begins studying at the secret "Floating University" of Warsaw.

Maria begins working as a governess to fund her sister Bronia's studies in Paris.

1867

1883

1884

1885

Maria graduates from high school and is awarded a medal for her academic achievements.

Maria Skłodowska is born in Warsaw, Poland, on November 7.

Maria falls in love with her cousin Kazimierz Żorawski, but his parents forbid their marriage.

Marie earns a master's degree in math, meets Pierre Curie, and begins researching magnetism in his lab.

Maria moves to Paris, France, to attend the Sorbonne University, changing her name to Marie.

1891

1893

1894

1895

Marie graduates from university with a master's degree in physics.

Marie marries Pierre Curie in July.

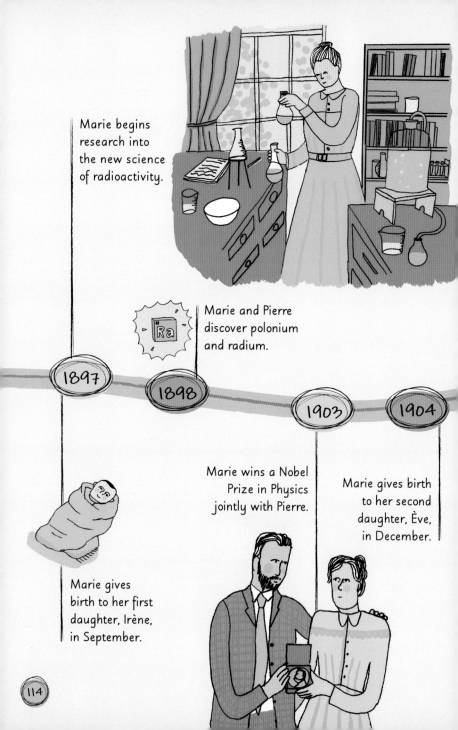

Marie begins research into the new science of radioactivity.

Ra

Marie and Pierre discover polonium and radium.

1897

1898

1903

1904

Marie wins a Nobel Prize in Physics jointly with Pierre.

Marie gives birth to her second daughter, Ève, in December.

Marie gives birth to her first daughter, Irène, in September.

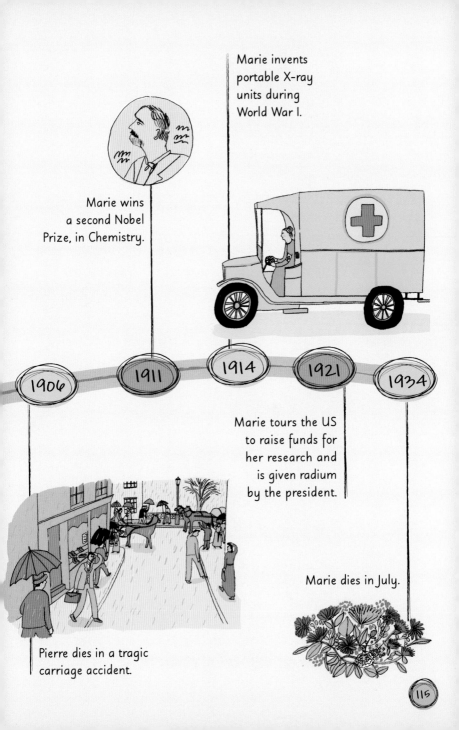

Marie wins a second Nobel Prize, in Chemistry.

Marie invents portable X-ray units during World War I.

**1906** **1911** **1914** **1921** **1934**

Marie tours the US to raise funds for her research and is given radium by the president.

Marie dies in July.

Pierre dies in a tragic carriage accident.

# Quiz

 What was Marie's nickname as a girl?

 What was the name of the secret university at which Marie studied in Warsaw?

 In which city is the Sorbonne University?

 How did Marie meet Pierre?

 What was Marie's first daughter named?

 In which rock did Marie discover polonium and radium?

 What contraption, invented by Pierre and his brother, did Marie use to study uranium?

**Do you remember what you've read?
How many of these questions about
Marie's life can you answer?**

 In which year was Marie awarded her first Nobel Prize?

 In which French city did Marie leave her stock of radium for safekeeping during World War I?

 What was the nickname of the portable X-ray units developed by Marie?

 Which US president gifted radium to Marie?

 Where are Marie and Pierre buried?

Answers on page 128

# Who's who?

**Becquerel, Henri**
(1852–1908) physicist who discovered that certain materials emit rays, later called radioactive rays

**Curie, Ève**
(1904–2007) daughter of Marie; she wrote a famous biography about her mother

**Joliot-Curie, Irène**
(1897–1956) daughter of Marie; she became a scientist and was awarded the Nobel Prize in Chemistry in 1935

**Curie, Paul-Jacques**
(1855-1941) Pierre Curie's brother; a talented physicist. Pierre and Paul-Jacques worked together to develop a type of electrometer, used in many of Marie and Pierre's experiments

**Curie, Pierre**
(1859–1906) husband of Marie and fellow scientist; he helped Marie make her discoveries of radium

and polonium and was jointly awarded the Nobel Prize in Physics for this work

**Dłuska, Bronisława**
(1865–1939) sister of Marie; she was also a physicist and helped set up what is now The Maria Skłodowska-Curie National Research Institute of Oncology in Warsaw, to research radium and later cancer

**Harding, President Warren G.**
(1865-1923) 29th president of the United States. Harding met Marie Curie at the White House during her tour of America and presented her with a gram of radium to aid her research

**Alexander II**
(1818–1881) Czar (emperor) of the Russian Empire between 1855–1881

**Przyborovska, Kazia**
(dates unknown) Marie's Polish schoolfriend. The two later exchanged letters about how much they loved school

**Roentgen Wilhelm Conrad**
(1845–1923) physicist who discovered X-rays

**Szczawińska-Dawidowa, Jadwiga**
(1864–1910) helped form Warsaw's secret Floating University, of which she was a student

**Skłodowska, Bronisława**
(1835–1878) mother of Marie and a teacher

**Skłodowska-Szalay, Helena**
(1866–1969) sister of Marie and an avid supporter of education for women; she set up a school for girls in Warsaw

**Skłodowska, Zofia**
(1862–1876 ) sister of Marie; she died when they were both children

**Skłodowski, Władysław**
(1832–1902) father of Marie; he was a teacher and was very proud of his country

**Skłodowski, Józef**
(1863–1937) Marie's brother, also a scientist

**Wierusz-Kowalski, Józef**
(1866–1927) Polish physicist, diplomat, and former tutor of Marie. He introduced Marie to Pierre Curie when assisting in her hunt for a laboratory space

**Żorawski, Kazimierz**
(1866–1953) Polish mathematician and cousin of Marie. The two fell in love while Marie worked as a governess for the Żorawski family

# Glossary

**cancer**
illness in which cells (building blocks of the body) begin to grow uncontrollably in the body, forming tumors

**chemical**
substance formed from particles that have reacted together

**chemistry**
scientific study of chemicals

**chemotherapy**
type of treatment for cancer

**dissolve**
when something breaks down into smaller particles

**element**
natural or artificial substance that can't be broken down into different materials

**emit**
release something, such as X-rays

**empire**
countries ruled over by the same leader

**experiment**
scientific test to prove a theory

**exposure**
being in contact with a substance

**Floating University**
organization teaching women secretly in Warsaw in the late 19th century; also called the Flying University

**formula**
mixture of ingredients needed for a chemical reaction

**government**
organization in charge of running a country

**institute**
school that specializes in an area of research

**invention**
a newly created thing, such as a piece of scientific equipment

**isolate**
to separate a substance from another substance

**laboratory**
place where scientific experiments are conducted

**lecture**
educational talk for students or the public

**magnet**
material that attracts metallic objects

**mineral**
naturally occurring solid or liquid substance

**master's degree**
secondary, advanced university degree, before a PhD

**physics**
scientific study of topics related to material structures and how the structures are held together

**pitchblende**
rock in which radium and polonium are found

**polonium**
radioactive element discovered by Marie Curie, named after Poland

**radiation**
rays of energy emitted by certain elements or materials they have interacted with

**Nobel Prize**
international prize awarded every year to people in different categories, such as physics, for excellent work

**penetrating**
passing into or through something

**Periodic Table**
grid of elements arranged by their number of atoms and properties

**PhD**
highest level of university education, in which someone gains the title "Doctor"

**radioactive**
emitting radiation

**radium**
radioactive element
discovered by Marie Curie

**research**
investigation of a subject

**scholarship**
award given to gifted
students, usually in the
form of money to help
them study

**Sorbonne**
ancient university in Paris,
France, famous for its
excellent teaching

**thorium**
element with a weak level
of radioactivity

**tuition**
payments that students have
to make to their universities
to study there

**uranium**
first radioactive element
to be discovered

**widow**
woman who has lost
her husband

**X-ray**
type of high-energy
radiation that can
pass through the body

# Index

# Acknowledgments

**The author would like to thank:** Kathleen Teece for her support and helpful editorial suggestions during the process of writing this book and to Irène Joliot-Curie for her biography of her mother.

**DK would like to thank:** Polly Goodman for proofreading and Helen Peters for the index.

The publisher would like to thank the following for their kind permission to reproduce their photographs:

(Key: a-above; b-below/bottom; c-center; f-far; l-left; r-right; t-top)

6 Alamy Stock Photo: Akademie / © ® The Nobel Foundation (bc). 7 Getty Images: Universal Images Group / Universal History Archive (crb). 11 Alamy Stock Photo: Lebrecht Music & Arts (t). 12 Alamy Stock Photo: Granger Historical Picture Archive, NYC (crb). 18 Alamy Stock Photo: Lebrecht Music & Arts (tr). 19 Getty Images: Hulton Archive / Fine Art Images / Heritage Images. 23 National Library of Poland (Biblioteka Narodowa, Warszawa): (clb). 24 Alamy Stock Photo: Lebrecht Music & Arts (t). 25 FOTOE: Cultural Communication (tr). 26 Alamy Stock Photo: Granger Historical Picture Archive, NYC. 29 Alamy Stock Photo: Active Museum / Active Art / Le Pictorium / Collection (cb). 31 Alamy Stock Photo: INTERFOTO / Personalities. 37 Alamy Stock Photo: Archive PL (clb). 38 Alamy Stock Photo: Photo12 Collection (tl). 39 Alamy Stock Photo: INTERFOTO / Personalities. 41 Alamy Stock Photo: IanDagnall Computing. 42 Alamy Stock Photo: Lordprice Collection (r). 49 Alamy Stock Photo: The Print Collector / Heritage Images (b). 52–53 Alamy Stock Photo: Science History Images / Photo Researchers. 54 Getty Images: Popperfoto / Paul Popper (tl). 57 Alamy Stock Photo: Archive Pics (bl); Science History Images / Photo Researchers (tl); INTERFOTO / Personalities (cr).

58 Dorling Kindersley: RGB Research Limited (clb). 63 Getty Images: Hulton Archive (b); Mondadori Portfolio (t). 69 Alamy Stock Photo: INTERFOTO / Personalities. 72 Alamy Stock Photo: Science History Images / Photo Researchers (b). 74 Alamy Stock Photo: Akademie / © ® The Nobel Foundation (crb). 75 Alamy Stock Photo: Universal Art Archive. 76 Alamy Stock Photo: Granger Historical Picture Archive, NYC (b). 78 Alamy Stock Photo: Everett Collection Historical. 80 Alamy Stock Photo: Science History Images / Photo Researchers (b). 84 Getty Images: The LIFE Picture Collection / Time Life Pictures / John Phillips (crb). 85 Alamy Stock Photo: Science History Images (t). 90 Alamy Stock Photo: Lebrecht Music & Arts (cb). 95 Getty Images: Popperfoto (cb). 96 Getty Images: Hulton Archive / Apic (b). 97 Getty Images: Popperfoto (cra). 99 Alamy Stock Photo: Glasshouse Images / Circa Images (b). 100 Alamy Stock Photo: Archive Pics. 101 Getty Images: Hulton Archive / Apic (crb). 102 Alamy Stock Photo: Gado Images / Smith Collection (tl); Hum Historical (br). 105 Getty Images: Universal Images Group / Universal History Archive (cb). 106 Alamy Stock Photo: Geoffrey Taunton (b). 109 Alamy Stock Photo: The Print Collector / Heritage Images. 111 Alamy Stock Photo: Granger Historical Picture Archive, NYC. (cl)

All other images © Dorling Kindersley
For further information see: www.dkimages.com

## ANSWERS TO THE QUIZ ON PAGES 116–117

1. Manya; 2. The Floating University (sometimes called The Flying University); 3. Paris; 4. He offered her space in his lab to work; 5. Irène; 6. Pitchblende; 7. An electrometer; 8. 1903; 9. Bordeaux; 10. *petite Curies* (little Curies); 11. Warren G. Harding; 12. The Panthéon in Paris